# ESTUARY

First published in 2026 by
The Dedalus Press
13 Moyclare Road
Baldoyle
Dublin D13 K1C2
Ireland

www.dedaluspress.com



ISBN 978-1-915629-52-4 (hardback)
ISBN 978-1-915629-53-1 (paperback)



Dedalus Press titles are available in Ireland from Argosy Books (www.argosybooks.ie) and in the UK from Inpress Books (www.inpressbooks.co.uk).

Cover image: *From Source* by Cora Murphy,
oil paint on canvas, 50cm x 40cm (WxH), 2024,
by kind permission of the artist.
www.coramurphy.com

Dedalus Press receives financial assistance from
The Arts Council / An Chomhairle Ealaíon.

the arts council an chomhairle ealaíon funding literature

# ESTUARY

PHILIP McDONAGH

DEDALUS PRESS

ACKNOWLEDGEMENTS

Some of the poems in this collection appeared in collections published by Ravi Dayal (New Delhi) and Rudomino (Moscow); in the *Irish Times, Poetry Ireland Review, The Clifden Anthology, Síolta,* and *Cassandra Voices;* in the anthologies *No Strangers Here* (Arlen House), *Cuban Love Poems* (Cassandra Voices) and *Head Over Heels* (Dara Foundation, Almaty); and in my adaptation into English of Nikolay Gumilyov's *Gondla* (Arlen House, 2016). I would like to thank my friend and fellow poet Pat Boran, Editor of Dedalus Press, for his kind, precise, and very insightful assistance in selecting the poems included here and in giving *Estuary* a structure.

# Contents

ENVOI

GHAZAL OF THE GENERALIFE AT DUSK

# PROLOGUE

# Estuary

At times, the birds act on one whim and migrate.
The reindeer armies darken the altogether
White tundra. And we humans make our moves
At one go; which can turn to an extreme
Event, a flash flood with panic and drownings.

The people who most fear loss are people like us.
We've worked hard, coding reality.
Our main ideas and manageable doubts
Are like big dams; the ebb and flow of thought
No longer decisive in any real sense.

Which means, at times the barrier to change
Is like a holdout, like a dam or wall
Waiting to crumble. But how things change becomes
At times creation, using every hand:
A source; and then the intricacies of sharing.

A river tumbles to the steadying sea.
The in-between world of a poem is like
The estuary, its muddy, dragging tide.
We're right and wrong, both: without self-hate,
We face the deficiency in how we live.

The helpful undercurrents, we pick up;
Phrases, then shades of colour, then a theme;
Our music is heard by all. We operate
In the disguised frontier between two prayers,
*Thy kingdom come;* on earth, *Thy will be done.*

As when prince Gondla chose love's open sea,
The currach of crystal and a green horizon.

Flash floods. Big dams. The ambiguity
Of estuaries. The uncovering of sources.
Unless there is something of the unexpected
In what happens, we won't know where we are.
Call it a voyage; call it baptism.

*Note: 'Estuary' was written as an opening chorus for my version of Nikolay Gumilev's 'Gondla'.*

# PART ONE
# A MAN IS HARDER THAN DIAMOND

# A Man is Harder Than Diamond

*for Ekaterina Genieva (1946–2015)*

*'Everything has become heavier and more massive; thus, man must become harder, for he must be the hardest thing on earth; he must be to the earth what the diamond is to glass. The sacred character of poetry arises out of the conviction that man is harder than everything else in the world'*
*—Osip Mandelstam, On the Nature of the Word (1922)*

Tverskaya; winter; Pasternak afraid.
You're known to be his friend. You're calling Stalin
a clown, a Cyclops, bully, murderer.
I didn't hear this and you never said it,
Pasternak whispers. Later, others as well
will say, 'How reckless is this Mandelstam,
and not even for one of his best poems.'
We didn't hear this and he never said it.

It started as a presence in the mind,
un-differentiated sound, a signal
calling for your attention. Out of this,
a kosmos with a pulse and meaning was born;
and when the poem was done and light broke,
you left it as it was, no more was needed.
By now inevitable, a formed image
above the formless dark, your statement stood.

Drunk on the wine of grace, you hazarded,
you and Akhmatova joshing like children
in Sheremetev's garden, cavaliers
holding the reins tight. I am ready for death.
And after this, and these unstoppable
words winging to the eaves of memory,

you're slopping out on an eastbound cattle-truck.
Your one possession is your immortal gift.

A transit camp; December; night has fallen.
By day, you slave with them carting rough stones,
now they're around you, ordinary thieves.
They want to give you bread and hear your poems.
Your yellow prison garb lit by a lamp,
the loft goes quiet. A dying nightingale,
you smile: 'Kamen, or Stone, was my first title.
Among Siberian stones, my last recital.'

The '60s; a commemorative reading.
The living cadences as intimate
as when the unborn moves within the womb,
as our denied souls. Word is going around,
Here in the hall, Nadezhda Mandelstam.
Chairs clatter, the engineering students turn.
I'm not, she murmurs, accustomed to panegyric.
At a mere lyric, they're cheering like hussars.

Doyen of the exposed, the uninsured,
of those who would speak a world into existence
having no title to even a single word,
you trusted, through the dead and deadening mist
of times of trouble, she ever would descend
and unbind speech, the table-turning Dove;
to share the bitter cost, that other Friend,
lender of last resort to all who love.

## Paradeisos

*What theme had Homer but original sin? – W.B. Yeats*

Denoting first *an area measured out,*
the classic *paradeisos* in Iran
meant refuge, a gardener's gamble in the desert,
relief of the burden-bearing caravan;

which speaks to us of that first Paradise;
of spontaneity, the peaches dripping
from trees, the rivulets; but equally,
of new ground broken, careful stewardship.

This Paradise was not a safe enclosure
for Adam to potter about in, trying to bell
the great cat of God with the mice of reason
as Eve hung round hugely available.

Our garden project had no *ne plus ultra.*
The problem was at base, the absorbing Tree
with properties that made a management
buy-out a seeming possibility

to the steward of the garden; and even then,
the deal presented as follow-through with her:
he slipped into the sweetly arbitrary,
Adam, who was the trusted arbiter.

The snake's démarche, our human hastiness,
did not mean 'heart' had triumphed over 'soul':
a sudden occlusion of wide-lensed reverence
by rampant privacy occasioned our fall.

# A Strange Mutation

*for David Donoghue, co-facilitator*
*of the UN Sustainable Development Goals (SDGs)*

'The only watchmaker in nature,' so
atheists write, 'is blind.' To go awry
not thinkable, things go as they will go:
no mind is implicit here, no mind's eye.

For poets dimly present on the scene
of politics, unheeded to, yet free,
the random, different operative gene
is the Darwinian analogy.

Nowhere was an imaginable mutation
as pregnant in the code, as among slaves.
Natural selection subjugated nation
to nation. Later, the withdrawing waves

of the Red Sea brought liberating battles
and new arrangements, but changed no one's mind
on using captured foreigners as chattels:
a bifurcation shredding humankind.

A once-off self-styled 'son of man' came touting
the poor, sharing their lives. Outside the gate,
we disappeared him, slave-wise, to efface
even his memory. To eliminate

the risk of nether-people logging in
to big ideas, was core; to declare
the element we exposed as carrion
a Mr. Nobody from God Knows Where.

So what on earth's going on, when we replace
long-tested notions with an un-Roman plan
*to reach the last first* – as if to embrace
the strange mutation of the Son of Man?

# No One Steps in the Same Riviera Twice

Caesar delivers the original
Riviera at the estimated expense
of one million dead among mere Gauls.
Posting on X 'To Connaught or to Hell',
a people-taming Force of Heaven cleanses
of reprobates our sodden-with-rain Riviera.
Rivieras on the Volga fill the brochure
Mein Kampf. The Congo is the heart of darkness,
so too the Putumayo. Wealth is blind:
investors picture them as new Rivieras.

No one steps in the same Riviera twice
or forever. All come undocumented,
all huddle on the Stygian Riviera.
In longing for the further shore, we stretch
our arms out. One who is not a dealer, this loser
from Galilee or Gaza, with his take
on money-changers, with his wounds, is there:
his gaze of mercy our one remaining hope.

# In the Museum at Hallstatt

At Hallstatt, window-pane to window-pane,
I pass through the museum of the Celts.
A leather basket. Tools for the salt-mine.
A brace of bracelets. Belts to end all belts.
Forget the bears' teeth and an iron sword,
these objects are the things we would learn to spell
in Irish class, our disregarded hoard.
There, jewels laid down as gifts at burial
prove all our grief, a silent literature.
And would I, prodigally, drop this whole thing
from torc to fibula for a self-sure
boot-fall, carved words, global positioning?
For what, in one last show-case, I see glint:
a bright sestertius from Vespasian's mint.

# Novgorod

*for Andrey Mashinyan*

The massacre Ivan the Terrible
commanded or condoned – was it for trade
or geopolitics or to instill
fear elsewhere? Was Novgorod unmade
merely for what she was – her free speech,
and her debating openly the claims
of kings? Or for her church domes, golden, reaching
elusively to heaven, like candle-flames?

# The Archway

A tracery in cobalt and dark lapis
fills the façade. Within the random night,
two tiger-suns rise up in symmetry,
the greatest and the greatest burning bright
above the archway; which an entire people,
abashed, abased, would pass through to parade
before the lame king; hidden within whose glamour,
the conscript lives, the slave-hordes, the price paid.

# The Lion and the Lamb

Ashoka needs an image he can rely on
to epitomize his reign:
on all his famous pillars he puts a lion,
apex of the food chain.

In due time, the mighty Mughals will depict
on their war-banners
a different lion; yet somehow contradict
themselves when their image-planners

picture a lion and a lamb at ease
with cherubs. *Satyagraha*
builds on this thought, disturbs old categories.
We litmus-test a law:

does the assertion of power, a lion-like feature,
allow the awareness, or sense
of the scenario, of a gentler creature?
For what is violence?

A traffic jam, a T-shirt, or a splat
of paint on the wrong side
of the enclosure, of some petty statute,
to highlight genocide?

Today, in the broad gap of danger
that is our planet,
to challenge is the part of a world-changer,
the part of woman or man.

*Satyagraha = Gandhian action in truth*

# The Futile Furore

In Hadrian's hunt,
a pulse of care
made me want
spear and arrow
stopped, an end
to blood-spattered sorrow,
an end to glory
without roots,
the futile furore.

We must adieu
the children,
though they die too.
May they yet live
in love, in light!
May they forgive
this wanting out
of our Princes'
terrible rout!

I credited,
we credit still,
in face of all dread,
that shape within
the stag's antlers
as the dogs drew in.
To suffer not do
the evil thing,
we stand with you,

whether you rest,
O Son of Man,
powerless
in Jerusalem;
or the great stone
rolled from the tomb.

*According to legend, the Roman officer Eustathius saw Christ's cross in the antlers of a hunted stag. As a result, he set limits to his obedience to the emperor Hadrian. Eustathius was later executed along with his wife and two children. In Rome, the church of Sant' Eustachio, surmounted by the sculpture of a stag's head, is a short walk from the Pantheon, the 'temple of all the gods' often cited as evidence of Hadrian's tolerance and sophistication.*

## An Impregnable Account

Uprooted from the world
as from a hostile womb,
his mind numbed
on milk that is no milk,
the captive, blindfold,
will plunge onto the rocks
and find oblivion.

Chapatis in their saddle-bags,
the messengers will ride
by sinuous tracks
to Delhi, Agra, Lahore,
disseminating
an impregnable account
of all that happened.

Mother of mosque and temple,
Ranthambore Fort
holds fast more victims,
a banner floating rigid in cold stone.

# Penelope

There in the harbour, an apron of dressed stone.
Odysseus is tossing orders to his men.
The urgency of doing has outgrown
All the old doubts. 'They may come not again
From Troy, these long–oared ships.' I could have died
Right on the spot. 'Await me until the day
The beard has come to that child's cheek.' *That child.*
'Then marry well.' And still he's looking away.

Waiting for sleep, my thoughts were numerous
As notes the nightingale produces, lonely
In darkness. Laneways near my father's house
Entered my dreams. Each morning there was only
Ithaca. The vague mist, the barren scree.
I too have wandered a weather–beaten sea.

## A Village Mass in Kerala

The chanted Malayali psalms begin
comforting hearts, the steady undertone
of a whole fishing village hauling in
truth beyond truth; and no one is alone.
Later, masala *chai*, the floating *diyas*
in their stone trough, the scent of frangipani,
a *thengu* tree. Branches out-splayed like stars
compel us gently with their testimony.

That poet of the misty mountainside,
on hearing Music, brought it down to earth
and moved among the rural poor, colliding
with their oppressors. A sense of self-worth
stirred within joy. So, may some Hesiod
complete our Mass; fix words on the malaise
of factory ships that steal men's livelihood;
align with reason all our Works and Days.

PART TWO

# A LOVER TO HIS BELOVED ABOUT LOVE

## A Lover to his Beloved about Love

*a ghazal after Firaq:*
*for Akhilesh Mithal (1926–2012)*

In this ruin somewhere
are some damaged earthenware
lanterns that we can find and light,
it being such a bad night.

# Milan, piazza Sant'Angelo, July 1978

The piazza by afternoon; a virginal day.
The *opere di restauro* are on pause.
Carnations bloom unchaperoned on their stall,
The *città lavoratrice* far away.

A friar in bronze completes the atmosphere,
except for a slow trickle from the stone
fountain that fills a bucket to overflow.
Into this moment neither here nor there

come raised heels and a girl whom Leonardo
might paint. Cool water, the opposite of silence,
would run in even one exchangeable word.

*Vuoi bere?* Her small dog gets his face wet,
guzzling. And there she waits. And there I am,
an image of the statue, a silhouette.

# November Days: 2010, 1879

*for Derek Mahon; after a painting by Levitan*

Hope under harassment; the Financial Times
all haircuts and insolvency regimes
and Irish taxpayers "thrown into debt-bondage;"
the snow of last night freezing on the ground
near Park Kulturi metro; we burrow in,
lodged in the world of Isaac Levitan.

What news can ever grieve this girl we see
striding an autumn path in Sokolniki
a hundred and thirty years ago, well-wrapped
in her scarf and purposes? How does it happen,
the instant owned – this freehold on the lease
of her prime beauty, among flaming trees?

We leave the Tretyakov to find fat sparrows
pecking on snow in the grass verge. Tomorrow,
my friend's look says, and winter will default
on frosty leaves, on all the bonds of autumn;
which notwithstanding, a November sun
somehow incurs no blame: our pulses run.

# Darshan

A cry, a spate of guessing,
this here-and-now supplanting everything,
this rush to cameras

to register a blessing:
the breaking surface of our dolphin-king,
beach-doyen, undreamt-of class.

We're in touch, on the go,
like children under the arm of a big wave,
slipping in swathes of foam.

Even on days of no-show
we were the better for the time we gave
hoping he'd come.

*Dars'ana, or darshan, is a Sanskrit term for the sighting, understood as an auspicious moment, of a deity or a holy person. The term has also been used to describe the way nature can present itself at certain moments.*

# At Ranthambore National Park, a Breeze Among the Pillars

*for Valmik Thapar (1952–2025)*

Here at a dusty crossing of the roads,
curious for contact,
we pass binoculars around.
A deer's cry in the forest,
the monkeys in cahoots, all frantic.
Then, the absolute insistence of a roar,
the lord of the melee of nature,
the tiger, orange ornament
of our deciduous world,
kaleidoscopic among trees.

We wait some more, put on our shawls.
A crocodile by water,
dead-like as the root
of the gnarled banyan.
The faint calls of doves.
Engine revved up,
the jeep moves on,
trundling through the retracting day.

I would acquire
a textual acquaintance with the leaves,
with the incorrigible modesty
of flame-in-the-forest;
with flights of parakeets
that spread in synchrony
in disappearing light
to settle all-in-one, a peacock's tail.

The *chhatri* on that slope
affirms, a breeze among the pillars,
the something that is ours
in all our passing.

# Russian Tradition

A young man shuffles backwards with a broom
dusting the footpath to prepare a way
for high-heeled bride and stiff grey-suited groom.
Some younger women, it being a summer's day,
kick shoes along the grass. One bright black shoe
lands like a gift from heaven at my feet.
'*Da. Russkaya traditsaya.*' On cue,
I look in her direction, our eyes meet,
her smile contains a thousand marriages,
different and all the same: this high June sun,
the padlocks promising no end of days,
the porch, the bonnets, the accordion.

## *Ormakkai*

*Far away across the ocean*
*underneath an Indian star*
*dwells a dark and lonely maiden*
*on the coast of Malabar*

The first song my soul made,
my song to remember you by,
is a song where every note is played
*ormakkai ormakkai.*

With you as friend, I would discover
the big path beyond my home.
Before the morning you were my lover,
the lines of life became a poem.

To every corner our questions led
and one by one the answers came,
a universe in what we said,
yet something was missing all the same.

Since of your going I heard it spoken,
my jar is broken, I draw no water.
For all that I'm a poor man's daughter,
I draw no water; my jar is broken.

The first song my soul made,
my song to remember you by,
is a song where every note is played
*ormakkai ormakkai.*

*In Malayalam, ormakkai translates as "memories" or "for remembrance".*

# Antigone and Pangur

канешна. Even factoring in
I'm Moscow-born, and feminine,
and non-white (more an orangey roan),
I identify with Pangur Bán,

first cat of the diaspora.
I mean, look. It isn't far
from a Carinthian monastery
to life in the OSCE.

A conscientious cat might lurk
by mouse holes to back up the work
of some monk; and what I do here
is help my non-cat overseer

by hiding in his briefcase, creeping
among his dictionaries to sleep,
or co-composing, treading back
and forth on our shared Apple Mac;

which can mean (maybe it's not great),
we neither of us concentrate
that much. Now Pangur and his monk –
clearly, I'd not want to debunk

either of them; it's not for me,
Russian-speaking Antigone
and of the new Irish, to anger
a colleague as well-got as Pangur

– but let me say just this: the pair
of them are Martha to our Mary.
Purring my way through a siesta
on my companion's broad chest,

I dream for his sake of a Big
Someone the sponsor of a gig
like this for him. We're great, us two,
with all this amazing stuff we do.

*канешна/kaneshna = of course/you got it.*

## The Nightingales

*a short elegy after Callimachus: for Clare Marx (1954–2022)*

A WhatsApp blurted out that you were dead,
Clare. And tears came. How often we looked ahead,
We friends! Our company outshone the sun,
Laying him down to rest. Now it's begun,
This after-time. But our home, still your home,
Like the atomic structure of a poem
Binds energy in. Your stance, your healing work,
Your nightingales, disprove the complete dark.

## Song of Autumn

*after Fina García-Marruz*

*Do you know the country? … Goethe*

It's never a great problem to revisit
Resorts of summer, of snows and glistening frost.
But where can I find mere ordinary words,
Your dark sweater, September's rustle and rust?
The truth, yes, I admire truth, plus the angels.
But what of the less true things that it was ours,
In all our scorching innocence, to uphold?
Not like some bold migration to the stars,
Those corridors in time in which we touched.
They had a nature that was all their own
To which I dream of rightfully returning.
But how, if the very country is unknown?
'Always' I write, and reference that dust:
The one who says good-bye says what she must.

PART THREE

# HORN AND IVORY

# As if the Land had Spoken

*'I know what I am doing, whether the white people like it or not'*
*—Edmund Burke, January 1786*

Out in the *Sundarban*, eight hours by boat
from Kolkata, we're hardly anywhere.
Rivers abut on swamp. No diplomat
has come this far within the unmapped mire
of mangrove and mud-flat since independence.
The voluntary staff and villagers
receive us on a patch of land suspended
under a white moon. Someone calls out "Sir",
a barefoot man in a white dhoti, all
eager to speak. "The Irish ambassador?
I come here as a teacher, a Bengali,
to thank you, sir – thank you for Edmund Burke."

As if the land had spoken, the reprise
of an old tale. Clubbable Company-men
mangling the story, harvesting rupees;
an advocate, a man of eloquence
drawing from wells of truth, doing what he can.
I hear a melody beyond space-time.
The ample channels of the *Sundarban*
run home to Ocean, the eternal stream.

## The Silence of the Moon

I knew that to control a regiment
I had to keep men always on the move,
their minds on ammunition; the intent,
the underlying game, not theirs to approve.

The dust of Kabul, a compound in Sudan,
the beach by Homer's Troy – one and the same:
under the useful silence of the moon,
one sailed or sallied out and made one's name.

At times, we simply gave more than we got,
the fury of the natives met our fury.
In Meerut, Lucknow, Cawnpore, Sialcot,
our bloody-mindedness was half the story.

Life in the service is a discipline.
A ranker learns his lines, the men who lead
extemporize wisely; the only sin,
fleeing the danger or flinching from the deed.

A dying soldier of both queen and king,
I made it to the Front. I looked on Dover,
our big canon boomed – the important thing,
the game was on still, though my part was over.

The armour of the tomb concludes the affair:
in grandeur in St. Paul's I lie interred,
an Irish dust that in the upper air
was *Earl of Kandahar and Waterford.*

# The Language of the Gun

How was the business to get going? Why doubt
Soloheadbeg? As revolutionaries,
we lit the fire that others had laid out:
a republic isn't based on the word 'please'.

We never saw it as wrong or underhand.
With other lads, I chanced it, went on the run,
and found a language the Brits would understand:
their own language, the language of the gun.

Why did their mothers let them join? To step
into a safe job and a uniform?
When we came on the scene, it was a *schlepp*
for those boyos to creep out of the warm

RIC nest. O but they had the gen
on what was tunnelling underneath – no daws,
policemen spying on other Irishmen.
Our operations were only for the cause.

I never so much as pinched a bicycle
in those days. When they edited
'My Fight for Irish Freedom,' they did well
to fix on that – they got inside my head.

Here in the States, I'm in with a new crowd,
not patriots – but it's a different scene,
and I get by. I won't say I'm not proud.
It took a hard man then. It took Dan Breen.

# John Hume, Public Representative

In the beginning was the word. In schools
the welfare state built, we in the Bogside,
the Glen, and Creggan got hold of mind's tools.
We walked in the daylight with a new pride.

Within stale boundaries, truth was by rote.
The drumbeat of our ahistorical
abstractions cornered us and crowded out
fresh instincts. Still, we held on. A rebellion

rooted in what a person sees beyond
present alternatives began to act
on others. Over time, knots were unwound.
Conflict became contingency, not fact.

John Hume, public representative:
once I had said it on live radio,
it marked me like a sacrament, as if
my life was not my own. I kept going

down all the years and on to Downing Street
and that last Passover; until it fell,
the old wolf-law. Yet who can explicate,
finally, great events in the detail

of one life? To remember bobs and bits
of ordinary decency is easier.
I crossed half the world for Ann Fitt's
funeral; it was winter, I was there.

# The Mockery

The lads knew all the risks. It helped our singing
together, on the run. The awful thing
was what it did to women. A full show,
the scourge, the nails, the end coming so slow
– for wife or child even to hear of it
was ruin. We in the movement did our bit
for condemned men, but stationing someone there?
The lads nailed up were usually past caring.
This pig of a hot day, I noticed one
woman who stood within just yards of her son
hoisted with our lads over jerking spears.
She told us later our dead volunteers'
questions – the choking words of men who lacked
everything – no, her son would not retract
friendship, though one poor lad may have lost his head.
*The real sin was the Roman show*, she said.
*Dogs' work. A mockery. A thing obscene.*
So yes, I do remember the Galilean.

# Deconstructing Silence

Silence they had construed as our consent:
the Romans never looked for some quintessence
of loyalty. Wrong though it may have been,
I took to that dull stage of the Sanhedrin,
performed a secondary part well, clung
to my effectiveness, and ruled my tongue.
No one could know the fears we left unsaid,
the brighter harbours that stayed unvisited.
With heavy calculations, we had laden
our word-carrying ships, no longer trading
in the untreated fact. Why choose to inflame
old injury, by giving truth its name?
The day good Nicodemus asked me come
join him and plead at the praetorium,
a noise that had been growing in my ears
through all the meetings and down all the years
turned into music. Something we made start
within the Roman governor's tomb-like heart.

# Renunciation

For such a big beginning, the hour seemed right:
the first day of the week, the end of night.
Today, the story has been written down,
this way or that; and though he said, 'tell no one,'
of certain things, I will spill out this much,
it knocked me back, the way he said 'don't touch;'
just like that other time in Capernaum,
he wasn't on the road, and yes, I saw him
as someone I could be with. 'If my right eye,'
he said, 'bathed in some brightness too nearby,
makes me shoot wide, forget even my aim,
better the eyes of ragged men and lame
who hit on the true mark.' I had tried to probe
towards who he was, put on him a royal robe,
for better or worse. That morning in the garden,
the truth came home to me. I felt his pardon
as I held back, and then the recompense
of mixing our two lives, in a new sense.

# Horn and Ivory

> *One is made of ivory, the other of horn [...] the dreams that pass through the gates of polished horn are fraught with truth ...*
> *—Odyssey, 19.634–8*

We were beginning to wonder, I won't deny it,
if in the end the authorities were right:
a destitute presenting as a king
was too outlandish, a dream transiting
the gate of ivory, we Greeks would say;
therefore, we left the city on that same day.
The stranger on the road with whom we shared
all this – how we'd backed off and hadn't dared
attend those meetings or commit to him
– stood still. He pointed out Jerusalem
as the sun set and quoted text on text
until we lost ourselves. Though not perplexed,
we had no words. The sorrow of the Messiah,
his gentleness, and how in Zechariah
he rides in wobbling on a donkey, seemed
obvious as a thing you knew you'd dreamed
and in the dreaming knew – as what we read
afterwards, in the breaking of the bread.

# The Choice of Medium

The slave is answerable in his body:
more than a maxim when you've seen the rod-
and scourge marks, the lifelong disfigurement
of man, woman, and child. With backs half-bent,
they kept old slave-stripes out of our eyes' way
in that assembly in Trastevere;
yet when I spoke of the devil as a ring
of lock-stepping souls, not crediting
the moves of mercy; as bloated prestige,
bustable power; and said his name was 'Legion',
our slaves made in the legionary wars
out East could only laugh. Before the applause
died down, the thing I asked our people to note
is how the Master, knowing the psalms by rote,
and every theory and every storyline,
chose for his medium the bread and wine:
Abraham's God, Isaac's and Joseph's God,
was answerable in this body and blood.

# Trojan Work

*for Gusty Spence, in memoriam*

Victoria by morning. Molyneaux
surveys the square,
the Palace wall for backdrop, his big show
hidden by mist. We say our separate prayer,

the Ulsterman with folded neat umbrella
advances. A short wait,
his finger like a dice-throw on the bell.
Our Taoiseach's handshake is robust as fate.

Mayfair at lunchtime. Edging slowly in,
this unionist MP.
His lateness tells how difficult it's been
to engage directly with the Embassy.

An Ulster veteran testifies, lock-jawed,
in Goring's dining room:
the Orange marched on many a long road,
to spare boot-leather he had stayed at home.

Slow autumn rain. An ivy-covered wall.
Ervine is reminiscing:
*To see the lights light up in College Hall*
*reminds me what went wrong, all that I missed.*

*We all go wrong*, I say. We're mulling over
the options for compromise;
his *fine if we can trust you* a breaking cover,
a visor lifted to reveal the eyes.

We know ourselves, not as Olympians
from zones of no care,
but Trojans, coursers weighted by our sins,
whose action in the mud of history is broken.

Then Gusty Spence, with me, a Myrmidon,
sits down when there is news
of peace; in a dark pub, his minders gone;
between us, two black pints and his tattoos.

*Abject and true remorse, that's what I feel:*
*abject and true remorse.*
Shadows are relegated by the real,
as far from windy Troy we take our course.

*At Whitesheets, my old father was in the party*
*that fired a gun-salute*
*at Willie Redmond's grave*. And in a heart
broken, there grew in that trench mud a root

of trust. *'A Catholic, a Southerner,*
*he saw him die. Me Da,*
*always in tears…'* I jump in to demur,
I say that Redmond's apologia

– that death, if death came, one day might assist
in reconciliation
– ended in nothing. *But the Loyalist*
*decision the other day on a cessation,*

I anyway ask, *by some thin corridor*
*connects to Flanders? Yes,*
comes the reply. From deep in family lore,
a phrase loved by our mother surfaces:

*So God spoke last.* With river-force, a drop
wells up, reveals the past
as raw stuff of the living art of hope.
Gusty completes the silence: *God spoke last.*

We mud-larks at a fancy starting price
hammer the heath of heaven,
pulling like Pegasus. Fresh form, to alight,
still travelling, on the azure plateau, is given;

in Trojan work, an echo from a deeper
valley; on our churned field,
substantial rain; the covenants we keep;
our acts of dedication, unrepealed.

PART FOUR

# BAI JUYI IN MOUNT LAVINIA

# Bai Juyi in Mount Lavinia

The morning after, life becomes too poor
to honour the flamboyant signature
of last night's fireworks. They've swabbed away
the spillage of the stars. It's New Year's Day.
Within the staidness of the business centre,
our last night's revellers are now intent,
in a reversal, on indexing life
to sports news, asset prices, global strife.
Their element is manageable stress.
The air-conditioning's magic breathing blesses
all smartphones, flower-shirts, bendy moccasins.
In this completed world, who has, wins.

A bench. Late evening warmth. I read Bai Juyi.
Wit, warnings, walkabouts, a way of seeing
the wide world. For our scripture, *the slow glory*
*of sunset, sea waves' ever-breaking story,*
*time uncontrollable and mixed with grief;*
*until the beauty in heron, lily, leaf*
*that almost has no name flairs and I find*
*that any who are mobbed or left behind*
*concern me closely.* Here is the terrain
where truth has chances, love is a campaign.
In the warm dusk, the viscous clarifies,
Lavinia's gardens take me by surprise.

# The Mausoleum of the Samanids

Out of the misty morning comes the proud
householder, a white-and-orange cat, to run
before us on the low precinct wall;
the carvings open up to a chaste sun.

This basket-woven look in layers of stone
is placid as we are, a down-to-earth technique,
until a rhythm picks up that veers towards heaven.
The pillars of the Parthenon still speak

for Pericles, this quiet *mazaar* brings back
a Persian dynasty. Great Avicenna,
on fire with learning in his library,
hunger in each traversal of his pen,

is one with the engineers whose intricate
channelling of scarce water by the art
of *qanat* eases burdens – old Bukhara,
learning and ingenuity both part

of prayer. 'And to this day,' our guide goes on,
'they make *ziyárat,* a local pilgrimage,
here to the mausoleum.' She points. A man
whose battered bicycle is on the edge

of the sparse lawn will tour the tombs on foot.
'A private thing, a child-birth it could be,
they bring to other saints. But when their need
falls in the sphere of civil society,

they turn still to the Samanids. For us,
a problem-solving justice is a sign
of holiness.' We see him now, our pilgrim,
statue-like, solitary in the shrine.

Those old school notes of half-a-century
ago come back to me, the teaching plan
of Father Redmond, his 'Avicenna, boys'
a shiver in the silk of Transoxiana,

preface to all-encompassing Aquinas
dropping the *Summa theologica*
because a sudden joy caused his life's work
'to seem, boys, in comparison, mere straw.'

Our pilgrim raises fingers to his forehead.
Our lowered eyes, his trusting supplication
that we now share, invite the stones to speak:
the whole *mazaar* an arrow in translation.

# A New Emoji for Hope

Invested by the snow, the great compound
of Suzdal lies inert. This ancient bell,
host once to all the villages around,
no longer corresponds from its tower cell.
Who can believe in the connectedness
of unobtrusive lives? More real are these
pings on our phone, our struggles to impress,
to pose, to choose, to fix our boundaries.

The slits are filled with light by a surprise
winter sun. A holdout for harmony,
a new emoji for hope. Snows downsize,
grasses return, tresses will grace the tree.
May friends in far time find in this old steeple
the home and hope and helpline of a people.

## *Meteōra*

The domes of Samarkand – gone for the day.
The starlings' volubility, a moon
disinterested, fill the observatory
ruins with life and lightness. We attune
to how, here, Ulugh Beg probed all belief,
prescinded from a spiritual self-will,
and took the stars' height. Galileo's grief
slips like attendant truth into the still
precinct. Here's Anaxagoras, on trial.
Too late; for he has aided Socrates
to wonder at, to love, this wandering file
of stars; which to be fearful of, appease
by offerings, is breaking trust with Mind,
sifting all things: for measurement and meaning
in how the heavenly bodies are aligned;
and for the swerve of hope always unseen.

*In ancient Greek, the meteōra are the heavenly bodies.*

# Ahimsa

For one glorious day
he wheels and dips and poses,
this tiger butterfly among the roses.
A gust would blow him away.

With a child's eye we perceive
his red-robed authority,
his lordship in a world that comes to be
not by our leave.

## Jasmine

On Vishnu's feast, cucumber and orange,
pineapple and pomegranate, unite in prayer.
Who can be sad or sorry,
seeing the jasmine in a girl's hair?
Why so busy and brutal
to achieve your purpose?
Krishna has his flute,
in Nature are a hundred thousand verses.

# Dome of the Minaret

*'We make the golden journey to Samarkand' – James Elroy Flecker*

*The acrobats of thought, for all their skill*
*in rope-work of the mind, will never scale*
*the dome of the minaret.* The morning mist
here in the Registan is like a veil
over our eyes. What does the inscription mean?
Is there some Persian wisdom or algebraic
equation that defies the acrobats?
Some tool, technique, or theory that they lack?

A crystalizing sun paints up the square.
A little girl is running, is about
to tumble. Her invigilating father
gathers her in, the shoulder of his coat
her dome beyond the world's pull-down. He turns
to acknowledge us. A smile, a quiet *'privyet'*
include us in the golden future tense
lived between Dad and daughter, *tète-à-tète*.

## Evening Raga on Lake Vembenadu

The houseboat's engine stilled, we can believe
ourselves a part of the ecology,
the water-hyacinth our prow will cleave,
this fading lamp above the Arabian Sea.

There's no technique to manhandle or stow
regularly a force that has no force –
the clouds, the cormorants, this overflow
of raga-music from an unseen source.

When David played for Saul in the old time,
Saul's inability to carry on
slowly dissolved. The right pause, a half-rhyme,
a word well-placed, is the criterion

or springboard of the new. Can we insist
on separated lives, we who agree
on what is beautiful? The scientist
whose job is to control salinity

and make the lake life-giving shares an agenda
with fishermen on tiny coracles
tossing out lines and raga players blending
with bird-cries and far temple-tethered bells.

# A Hindu Prayer

However well begun,
said Mr. Subramanian
to our two girls,
all work needs God.

In people's lives, care,
a weight of suffering, is there
always. An act of mercy
lessens the load.

You never know the day
life ends. Always pray.

# The Ends of the Earth

*for Brendan McCarthy*

These marginals, the makers of *mithai*
and bangles, shoeshine wallahs, rickshaw-men,
their dull brown blankets like crab-shells,
fade into doorways in Calcutta rain:
whole ladlefuls in every sink and gutter
make them extinct almost, lost in the deluge.

The lights are out, the city's power-failure
matched by a power-failure of the moon.
'Where you or I are one – bold in our purpose
– these poor are a thousand-fold, exist, it seems,
by a mere chance.' Mid-slum, mid-slur of rain,
we walk on, on some infinite descent.

My guide is Dr. Brendan, renegade.
'I left the Christian Brothers, I mean their house,
to start SERVE, a helpline for young people.
My colleague Kevin does the railway platforms.'
Ends-of-the-earth. A giant tenement.
The rain conceals the courtyard like a curtain.

Inside, for chairs, arrangements of old boxes.
For pictures, cuttings out of magazines
with rims of cellotape. 'To do the platforms?'
'To gather up the dying is what it means.
Our helper is from Japan. No religion.
He does this on his holidays each year.'

Desk. Telephone. Computer. A portrait
above the desk: Edmund Ignatius Rice.
'A child should always have a place to turn.'
As if he clutched a stalk, a spark stolen
from heaven, and One more powerful than the rain
protected in His palm the guttering flame.

# PART FIVE
# THE SEQUEL

# The Sequel

*for Kilian McDonagh, on his 21st birthday*

We hardly see it, the rare light of the stars,
there for us as we begin
singing our songs: Tralee and Malabar,
Yeats and Kavanagh and Shane McGowan.
The cake turns into crumbs among the cans
of Heineken; until, as if from nowhere,
our twenty-somethings with accuracy are chanting
a version that is theirs
from schooldays of 'The Holly Bears a Berry,'
their swing, their steady beat,
so white, so black, so red, so ordinary,
we find a focus, though eyes do not meet.

On impulse we all rise:
the star-filled night
has trodden on the heels of morning.
Time for goodbyes.

Then Kilian, seventeen,
on a borrowed bicycle and an ounce of sleep,
goes down to *Pointe* in the vivifying
earliest morning air, and from this trip
in which he casts his line out into the milling
Atlantic, appears back bright as a spinner
not for, but with, his breakfast. A silver
trophy, a worthy winner.

Except, the contest never was,
only abundance,
his grabbing the handlebars at dawn,
action without a cause.

# The Shining Snow

No skis or ski-boots in the resort shop
to match her small size. Others go on ahead,
drag-lifted to the sunlight at the top.
For her, tobogganing in a slushy meadow.
Her tears in spate occur by the cold pylons,
for nothing almost, nothing that can be spoken
– the bow-sweep of their skis, a stamp, a style,
that full shilling beside the doubtful token
of one small person unsure of where she is.
An agile ski-instructor, taking this in,
lifts her and carries her through lines of trees,
by T-bar, to the summit. Citizen,
now, of the realm of shining snow; and strong
in just being part of it, the mere belonging.

# Omphalos

Tara is ten, Diya near nine.
It's our big trip to Istanbul.
The waters of the Golden Horn
glimmer for us at noon. As fine
as banqueting, this open stall,
one-euro punnets of salted corn.

On Day Two, Hagia Sophia
fills half the sky and all my head.
Nearby, a splurge of minarets,
is the Blue Mosque. Here Tara and Diya
become past reason interested
in any and every passing cat.

Cats are a thing. Along the coast
in Bodrum, we awake one day
to find in occupancy downstairs
what Jonathan, our generous host,
expressly forbids: a couple of stray
beach-cats, as if the couch were theirs.

Off Bodrum beach, a catamaran
tracks Tara on the trembling foil
that to her Dad's the Aegean Sea.
Our *omphalos* is that *she can*,
grappling with a flappy sail,
zigging her zags intuitively.

# The Two Musketeers

*for my god-daughter Lilah Singh*

Great–grandfather came home from serving France,
and having seen the explosions, the bladed guns,
vowed never again to enter a church and pray.

The western front, vengeful Versailles. Beside
our haveli gate, an untouched refuse heap
speaks of that world of untouched consciences.

Delicate as a butterfly, the sunbird
explores hibiscus blossom, and I dream.
Lilah is of the Punjab and of France.

When Europe's eldest daughter France engages
*Bhāratavarṣa*, and they commit themselves,
the musketeers of global dialogue,

truth as their rapier, to cry out '*en garde*'
to arbitrary force, to lawless markets,
to media that crush the demotic word,

see, he will bless our Salt March to the future,
that old soldier who would accompany
a dear, frail, valiant wife to the church door.

*Bhāratavarṣa or Bharatavarsha is a Sanskrit name for India understood as a civilisation, not a state.*

# Above Death's Precipice:
# a Song for the Scattering of Ashes

*for Naomi Judah-Good (1918–2022)*

I

Out of a navigational
instinct, gather we must.
But what's the story that we tell
to disappearing dust?

Which is more real? The thing or force
depriving us of you,
dear Naomi, that lurch of chaos
pretending to be true?

Or years of friendship, affirmation,
shared meals, old recipes?
The poems we loved in this hard station
above death's precipice?

II

The details of that story are unsure.
And so we sing down all the years
songs of shared laughter and shared tears,
the golden songs that still endure.

# The Consolation of the Common Life

We found it once under the Christmas tree,
in things as manifold as a box-kite,
an orangey car and Wilbur the Buzzing Bee:
extra, unbudgeted, ours as of right.

It came too like the swirl of a soft breeze
when the older ones on a slow afternoon
forgot their Leaving Cert to organize
all the young cousins in a game of Cluedo.

All those shirts (Ana has packed my case)
perfectly folded in that way of hers
with cufflinks, ties – they look me in the face,
more than the sum of their particulars.

To ride on Feichín's boat, we jettison
papers and projects. Out in Galway Bay,
we see the Caorán Beag glow in the sun,
as if to see the world on the seventh day.

Each morning now, Bob is contributing
as Bobby or Sunny gives the crossword clue;
and late at night, he's part of the whole thing,
leads in reciting 'Dangerous Dan McGrew.'

A break from 'Hallelujah' on the guitar.
Here's Ana's apple crumble and a knife
and whipped cream. In one small agora,
the consolation of the common life.

# The Love Letter

Cornmarket on Saturday. A city fends
for itself. Townspeople debouch
from Lyons, the Golden Cross.
In a corner of their English battlefield,
Salvation Army trumpets
joust with Mammon.
As if the day had been too hot,
as if we had always belonged here,
the silence of a quadrangle,
then of another quadrangle,
welcomes us to my room:
my Dad, the Irish civil servant;
my immigrated cousin Dan;
myself, a third-week, first-term student.

Even now, I'm just that bit afraid
of first-class carriages,
the lobbies of the best hotels,
sacristies, solicitors' waiting rooms.
Oxford was like that for us,
though Staircase 15
might make one think otherwise:
the narrow bed, a gas fire, a chest of drawers.
That afternoon I boiled a kettle,
the three of us had Nescafe
and Jacob's biscuits.
Then, on a Hacker radio
my uncle Phil had given me for Oxford,
I made them listen to a race
from Newmarket:
that other England,
that spiritual landscape

where casting for the Irish roles
was further advanced.

Before too much was said,
we left Balliol,
its ancient stones, unlikely promises,
and in the rain that had fallen steadily
since the Middle Ages,
we took a taxi out beyond the colleges
to Oxford Station.

It was an elemental station then,
more station than shopping mall.
There was a footbridge,
and if you carted more books
in your suitcase
than you really needed,
it calloused your hands.
That was the bridge
from which Dad waved,
me smiling an end-stopped smile,
the rain still darkening the afternoon.

An hour later I was on my way
to where I am now.
Shoulder to gowned shoulder
at college dinner, I had paid
three shillings worth
in blue tickets. A small turn-out
it being Saturday,
but there was still the avidness,
the buzz continuing
in Balliol Junior Common Room
over milky coffee,
among punched-up newspapers.

A footbridge framed in memory like a picture.
A Father Waving Goodbye.
Call it an inscription
that I decipher
with a newly discovered key.
Or see me as an African
who after many years
of trading up and down the white man's coast
discovers the real exchange rate of gold.

What I know as I look back
on those transactions
of half a century ago
is that the day the great Nijinsky,
produced by Lester at the Bushes,
failed to reel in Lorenzaccio
up the hill;
which means a Saturday
in October 1970;
that same day on the train to Paddington
my Dad was cut off by the tide
that comes always unseasonable
to presage the unwinding of past worlds.
To see me silent under English rain,
who had once tottered through the living room
at arm's reach,
was seeing the circle of the family
disturbed like a bird's nest
or like a ceremony
no longer conjuring dreams.

Humanity is born to look up.
Walking the length of that obscure
platform at Paddington,
my Dad must have looked up,

and seen Brunel's ribbed vault,
a heaven that takes its colouring
indifferently from day or night,
a temple roof with no place for an altar.

Later, from a small hotel room,
he will write me the longest letter
he ever wrote, the largest share of him
I ever had, with ideas and jokes
I was to make a fist of, make my own,
half-child on the floor of the Oxford Union.

I rise to speak. The motion is,
*That God is a public school man.*
'Do we accept,'
I ask, drawing on Dad's notes,
'God's omnipresence, God's omnipotence?'
That term's President
Eric Parsloe, who left home at fifteen,
an older student, a trade unionist,
takes me aside.
'No need for politicking.
You'll be the President one day,
speaking like that.'
As if it were my calling.
As if he had known
a fact beyond phenomena,
that something is born of nothing.
A sunburst from a father's heart
empty as a magician's hat.
A maiden speech studded invisibly
with every last accoutrement of love.

# Circus in Lettermullen

Tonight in Lettermullen, next in Spiddal,
or Clifden, from town to town
they celebrate, like Raftery the fiddler:
ponies, acrobats, the Hungarian clown.

It's partly zany – the clown is up a lamppost,
his braces catch, the things he's carrying,
too many parcels, flee from his arms and burst
– and partly grave: the ring

darkened, a duo from Ukraine will shove
off, ready to stake limb
and life in the arc of white light above:
a small kiss on the neck from her to him.

For five-year old Diya,
my knee becomes a ringside seat, her throne.
And Tara, seven, her hair squashed on my ear,
whispers, *What next?* We're in the crowd alone.

Against the darkness, a tarpaulin tent;
artists and jugglers, merchants of candy-floss;
a pop-up monument,
where for an endless instant our lives cross.

*envoi*

# GHAZAL OF THE GENERALIFE AT DUSK

# Ghazal of the Generalife at Dusk

*for Ana*

Ignoble sparrow,
pale as the paving stone,
no tomorrow,
no defeat or bygone,
wrenches
your quiet adventure.
You touch our shared earth
for these few seconds
at merciful dusk.
Picking and pecking
at worm, seed, husk,
you know your worth.

Your fly-about
you spin out.
As a pattern multiplies
on clay tiles,
you flit, you settle.
A breath of wind, cool
in the latticed roof,
means as much or as little.
Streams of paradise
are not more silent.
A moon above the abyss
disturbs less.

*The Alhambra – perfection*
*never to be attained*
*by the striving, sombre*
*horseman of the plains …*

You, sparrow,
have a narrower
take on this:
a huge hypothesis,
born of what prophets tell
and human reasoning,
is native and natural
as dust shaken from the wing.

Time's arrow
fallen from the air,
you're neither here nor there,
dull sparrow.
On how it ends,
nothing depends,

Except in one sense:
the Architect
of the Garden
marks your fall;
and we, in consequence,
expect
peace, pardon,
and at the end of all,

the Sea where to depart is to arrive
and being remembered is to be alive.

www.ingramcontent.com/pod-product-compliance
Ingram Content Group UK Ltd.
Pitfield, Milton Keynes, MK11 3LW, UK
UKHW041137230426
470288UK00007B/39

9 781915 629531